homeowner's
RECORD KEEPER

THE PERFECT PLACE TO KEEP TRACK OF HOME REPAIRS, MAINTENANCE, PLANS, AND DREAMS

christina henry de tessan

CHRONICLE BOOKS
SAN FRANCISCO

I am Hoping that this book will help my children when they are in charge of ferry cliff

ISBN 0-8118-3828-5

Design by Alethea Morrison

Cover illustration by Maria Carluccio

Manufactured in China

Distributed in Canada by

Raincoast Books

9050 Shaughnessy Street

Vancouver, B.C. V6P 6E5

10 9 8 7 6 5 4 3 2 1

Chronicle Books LLC

85 Second Street

San Francisco, CA 94105

www.chroniclebooks.com

INTRODUCTION

It is such a thrill to turn the key in the lock, push open the door, and step across the threshold of your own home. You are master of your domain, giddy with the reality of claiming a few walls and the roof over your head as your very own. You can paint those walls any color of the rainbow and not have to justify your whims to some uncomprehending landlord whose only care is that the rent gets paid on time. Whether you are a first-time home-owner or have owned a home before, this is your chance to shape your living space into something suited to your own lifestyle and needs.

All that said, home ownership is a long and demanding relationship. For just as there is no longer any need to ask the landlord for permission to paint your bathroom canary yellow, there is also no one to call when the toilet overflows on Christmas Day. Instead of going for a bike ride on a sunny Saturday afternoon, you may find yourself at Sears, debating the merits of side-loading versus top-loading washing machines. Your house may be littered with paint-chip samples from Home Depot and stacks of papers that you know are important but don't know where to keep. You suddenly own not only the house itself, but a great many appliances and systems to which you've never given much thought but which are lurking behind those walls and under the floors—and are certain to demand your attention in the years to come. Something as seemingly mindless as maintaining a comfort-able room temperature involves several appliances that you must own and maintain.

Home ownership is heady stuff at first, but without proper care and organi-zation, it can become overwhelming—and can make you feel like your home owns you rather than the other way around. This record keeper is designed to help you organize, prevent, and plan ahead. Your house is likely to be the biggest investment you ever make, and you owe it to yourself to take care of it. Used properly, this journal will save you time in the years to come and spare you the hassle of reinventing the wheel every time a problem presents (or *re*-presents) itself—and they *will* present themselves. The records you keep here will help you assert some control over the logistics of maintaining your home.

This journal is divided into two sections. RECORDS will help you keep track of the past and current state of affairs: work that has already been done, appliances you already own, current paint colors, and routine maintenance. The second section, PLANNING, is designed to help you look ahead: *Resources and Inspiration* gives you a place to dream, sketch, and paste clippings as you try to figure out what you want. The *Goals* and *Worksheets* pages will help you prioritize and plan for those inevitable repairs, maintenance tasks, and improvements.

The most important question perhaps is: Why? Why bother tracking all this information, keeping every receipt, filling in all these sections—aside from a sort of vague sense that it's the responsible thing to do?

First of all, organization is the best weapon against disaster and frustration. Anticipating the needs of your house and keeping careful records will help you avoid some of the common perils of delayed or inconsistent maintenance, muddled planning, and confusion over what materials were used or when work was last done. Although at first it may be easy to remember when you replaced the furnace filter or last had the chimney cleaned, as you cycle through the years it gets harder to remember those kinds of details. Routine maintenance is difficult to keep track of and too important not to.

Second, remember that you will probably own your house for many years, and the world around you is constantly changing. Companies go out of business or get bought up; people change jobs or move away. You are the only one who can provide continuity over time. If you don't have records of what was done, which materials were used, or how a problem was solved, the next person you hire will have a harder time fixing it.

Third, good records will give you a sense of the myriad expenses that you'll rack up over the course of a given year, enabling you to plan ahead and budget more accurately. You can't entirely eliminate the unexpected, but you can begin to plan for the more predictable costs of upkeep.

Tracking the many repairs, maintenance needs, and improvements your home requires can also alert you to whether a repair job was done incorrectly or whether an appliance is causing more trouble than it should. You won't necessarily know (and won't be able to prove) that you bought a lemon unless you can produce proof of repairs. If your roof starts to leak, you'll want to be able to check when the job was done and whether it's still under warranty.

Finally, good records are absolutely essential if you ever plan to sell your house. Your tax advisor will want to know every detail of what went into renovating and improving your home, and any potential buyers will feel more confident if you can provide details of what was done when. In addition, if you receive rental income from your property, you are entitled to certain tax deductions on building upkeep, so you'll want a clear record of those.

In each section, you will find general tips, questions to ask, and suggestions for how to think about a project, all of which will help you consider your options. In most cases, however, your projects and repairs will require further research. The local public library is a great place to acquaint yourself with what might be involved in a given project—whether you plan to sponge-paint the living room yourself or need to find out what questions to ask roofing contractors. Ask friends and neighbors for suggestions about how they handled a given problem. Several Web sites also provide invaluable information (thisoldhouse.com, doityourself.com, oldhouseweb.com, naturalhandyman.com, to name just a few), and the numerous television programs devoted to home improvement are another good source. Countless home-improvement books line the shelves of bookstores, but be realistic about how much of the work you intend to do yourself before investing in a slew of how-to books. Finally, much as you may want to ignore them, the owner's manuals of your appliances provide important care and maintenance information.

Whether you have grand home-improvement dreams or simply want to take care of your home, good maintenance habits will save you time, money, and frustration in the long run. By thinking ahead and keeping good records, you will be well on your way to a happy relationship with your home.

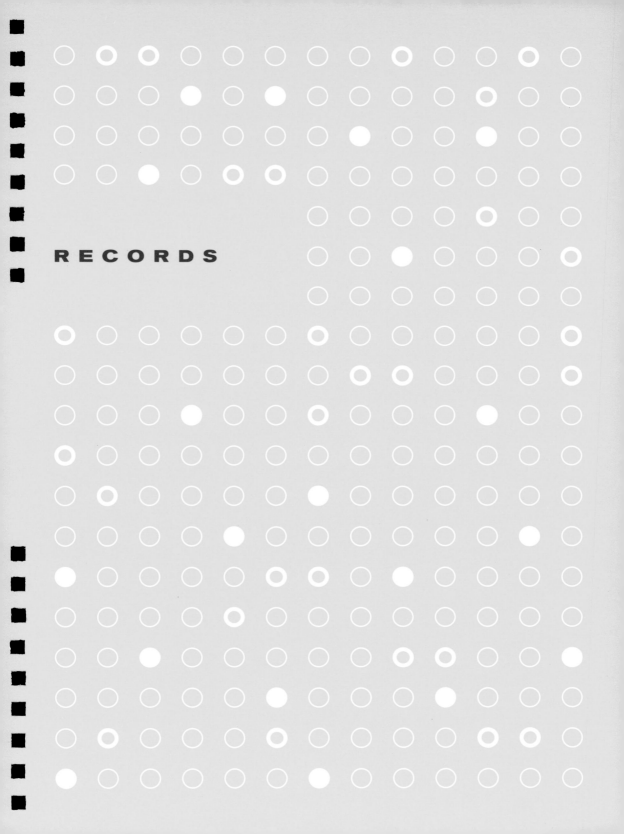

RECORDS

key contacts and information

MORTGAGE COMPANY >

None

contact >

address >

phone >

fax >

e-mail >

web site >

account number >

notes >

HOMEOWNER'S INSURANCE COMPANY >

contact >

address >

phone >

fax >

e-mail >

web site >

account number >

notes >

HOME SECURITY COMPANY >

None

contact >

address >

phone >

fax >

e-mail >

web site >

account number >

notes >

ELECTRIC COMPANY >

Fox Islands Electric Co.

address >

phone >

web site >

account number >

notes >

key contacts and information

GAS COMPANY >

Vinalhaven Fuel

address >

phone >

web site >

account number >

notes >

GARBAGE COMPANY >

—Dump — Airport Rd.

address >

phone >

web site >

account number >

notes >

RECYCLING COMPANY >

Take all trash to dump

address >

phone >

web site >

account number >

notes >

WATER COMPANY >

We have our own well. outside back door

address >

phone >

web site >

account number >

notes >

key contacts and information

TELEPHONE COMPANY >

contact >

address >

phone >

fax >

e-mail >

web site >

account number >

notes >

LANDSCAPING/LAWN MAINTENANCE >

contact >

address >

phone >

fax >

e-mail >

web site >

account number >

notes >

ARBORIST >

contact >

address >

phone >

fax >

e-mail >

web site >

account number >

notes >

HOUSE CLEANING COMPANY >

contact >

address >

phone >

fax >

e-mail >

web site >

account number >

notes >

key contacts and information

CONDOMINIUM ASSOCIATION >

contact >

address >

phone >

fax >

e-mail >

web site >

account number >

notes >

ARCHITECT >

contact >

address >

phone >

fax >

e-mail >

web site >

account number >

notes >

INTERIOR DESIGNER >

contact >

address >

phone >

fax >

e-mail >

web site >

account number >

notes >

GENERAL CONTRACTOR >

contact >

address >

phone >

fax >

e-mail >

web site >

account number >

notes >

key contacts and information

FLOOR INSTALLATION COMPANY >

contact >

address >

phone >

fax >

e-mail >

web site >

account number >

notes >

FLOOR REFINISHING COMPANY >

contact >

address >

phone >

fax >

e-mail >

web site >

account number >

notes >

PROFESSIONAL CARPET CLEANER >

contact >

address >

phone >

fax >

e-mail >

web site >

account number >

notes >

GENERAL HANDYMAN >

contact >

address >

phone >

fax >

e-mail >

web site >

account number >

notes >

LOCAL HARDWARE STORE >

contact >

address >

phone >

fax >

e-mail >

web site >

account number >

notes >

LOCAL BUILDING SUPPLY STORE >

contact >

address >

phone >

fax >

e-mail >

web site >

account number >

notes >

LOCAL NURSERY >

contact >

address >

phone >

fax >

e-mail >

web site >

account number >

notes >

PAINTER >

contact >

address >

phone >

fax >

e-mail >

web site >

account number >

notes >

PLUMBING SERVICE >

contact >

address >

phone >

fax >

e-mail >

web site >

account number >

notes >

EMERGENCY PLUMBING SERVICE >

contact >

address >

phone >

fax >

e-mail >

web site >

account number >

notes >

ELECTRICAL SERVICE >

contact >

address >

phone >

fax >

e-mail >

web site >

account number >

notes >

SWIMMING POOL SERVICE >

contact >

address >

phone >

fax >

e-mail >

web site >

account number >

notes >

FIREWOOD SUPPLIER >

contact >

address >

phone >

fax >

e-mail >

web site >

account number >

notes >

CHIMNEY CLEANING COMPANY >

contact >

address >

phone >

fax >

e-mail >

web site >

account number >

notes >

HEATING AND A/C SERVICE >

contact >

address >

phone >

fax >

e-mail >

web site >

account number >

notes >

PEST CONTROL SERVICE >

contact >

address >

phone >

fax >

e-mail >

web site >

account number >

notes >

HOME INVENTORY > It is vital that you create a home inventory that itemizes the contents of your home and their value, and that you keep a copy of this document off-site (in a safe-deposit box, for instance), so that you can gain access to it should something happen to your home. You can also keep it in a fireproof safe, but if you keep the safe at home, have it bolted down. Keep the following tips in mind as you prepare to inventory your home.

As you compile your list, don't simply write "TV." Note the brand, year it was purchased, retail price, size, and serial number. If you own any valuable art, get it appraised and keep the appraisal in a safe place. If you own jewelry or home office equipment that exceeds your insurance policy's standard coverage, take out additional coverage.

These days you can prepare an inventory in any number of ways. Some people walk around their home with a video camera, describing the details of each item as they survey the room; others take photos with a digital camera and download them to a computer or Web site. Another modern-day solution is to e-mail the list and photos to yourself or a friend. Good old-fashioned pen and paper are effective as well. The important thing is to get around to doing it and to keep the list in a safe, accessible place. Remember to update your inventory annually. It won't do you much good to pull out a list of items whose most recent entry is 15 years old.

HOME INSURANCE POLICY > Keep a copy of your home insurance policy in an easily accessible file so that you can refer to it when you purchase something new. Your insurance company will also have a copy on hand, but you should keep a copy in your fireproof safe or safe-deposit box nevertheless.

MAJOR REPAIR, RENOVATION, OR ADDITION > Get a copy of the building plan, septic tank location, and drain field for your property from the county before proceeding with any major repairs, renovations, or additions to your home.

DEEDS > If you are paying off a mortgage, your bank is currently holding the deed to your home. When you pay off your mortgage and you have the deed in hand, file it away in your fireproof safe or safe-deposit box.

RECEIPTS AND SUMMARIES FOR REPAIR OR ANNUAL MAINTENANCE WORK > Keep all receipts and summaries in case you come to suspect later on that a faulty job was done; to remind yourself what exactly was done and what it cost; or to show potential buyers you kept a pristine maintenance record. When you can't remember what finish was used on your new floors and the company that did the job has gone out of business, you will want to have the original letter of agreement as a record of what was done.

RECEIPTS FOR ALL MAJOR HOME IMPROVEMENTS > Keep these in a file for tax purposes. When you sell your home, you will not have to pay capital gains taxes on any major home improvements, so it is important to keep these papers in order.

WARRANTIES > File these in an accessible location with their receipts and the owner's manuals.

COST SPREADSHEET > You should create a spreadsheet to track your home-related expenses. There are numerous computer software packages to help you sort out your financial life, but even the simplest handwritten record of costs will help you budget more precisely in the future and will be of interest to potential buyers.

In one pocket of this record book, keep receipts for work that has recently been done. Transfer the receipts into a file on a regular basis, first noting on your spreadsheet all the costs and, in the relevant section of this book, the nature of the work done. The other pocket is designed to help you store papers regarding upcoming and current projects.

Remember to go through receipts and warranties periodically and throw out any that have expired, as well as ancient utility bills. It is worthwhile to keep utility bills for comparison's sake from one year to the next and in case a potential buyer is curious, but it is unnecessary to keep everything forever and it only creates clutter.

PAINT SWATCHES > Tape or staple swatches of the paint you use in the appropriate sections of this book, and you will never again be left guessing— not only what the exact color is called, but also what finish or brand you used. Although these things always seem obvious at the time, remember that home ownership is a long-term commitment. It may be difficult to recollect the data on the exterior trim color 10 years down the road when it comes time to repaint, and if you are simply repairing a ding in the wall, it will save you time to have the relevant information about the paint close at hand.

If you choose to use this worksheet, be sure to photocopy additional pages before filling it out.

DATE:

ITEM >

value >

details >

ITEM >

value >

details >

ITEM >

value >

details >

ITEM >

value >

details >

ITEM >

value >

details >

ITEM >

value >

details >

ITEM >

value >

details >

ITEM >

value >

details >

When it comes to home ownership, you simply can't afford to ignore routine maintenance, much as you may be tempted. First of all, and most important, preventive maintenance ensures that your home remains a safe place to live. Second, it is crucial to preserve your investment. Finally, you will avoid bigger headaches and bills in the long run by increasing the longevity of your appliances and systems and solving problems before they turn into full-scale disasters. A leaky faucet or running toilet will consume hundreds of gallons of water over time; dried-up caulking will cause mildew and rot, which can lead to structural damage. Use the pages that follow to keep track of repairs, maintenance, improvements, and changes you make over the years.

In addition to the following maintenance checklist, do a general survey of the interior and exterior of your home once a year. Inspect the roof and make sure it is clean. Check the foundation, roof, and siding for cracks. Check that doors to the exterior and windows seal properly, and inspect all walls and ceilings for cracks or evidence of leaks. Keep an eye out for the unexpected: a little pile of dirt on the floor could be the first visible sign of termites; if a given room or area smells musty, look for dry rot; droppings may be a sign of mice. Pay attention to things that don't look quite right, and investigate.

Preventive care is all too easy to neglect, what with all the more urgent demands of daily life. If you have trouble remembering when to do certain things, mark them in your calendar or link them to other annual events: When you turn the clocks back in the fall, it's time to have the chimney cleaned. When the kids go back to school in September, it's gutter-cleaning time.

PROJECT	TIMES / YEAR			
Remove debris from gutters and downspouts and ensure they are securely attached	❑			
Get chimney cleaned	❑			
Clean or replace furnace filter	❑	❑	❑	❑
Have furnace professionally inspected	❑			
Clean or replace air-conditioning filter	❑	❑	❑	❑
Have hot-water system professionally inspected	❑			
Clean and seal deck; check it for rot	❑			
Vacuum vents and coils of refrigerator	❑	❑		
Vacuum lint from dryer; clean out duct and vent	❑			
Check septic tank level	❑			
Clean stove vent and fan	❑	❑		
Check caulking in bathrooms	❑			
Check smoke detector batteries	❑	❑		
Inspect worn fittings and hose connections on all appliances that use water	❑			
Change oil in lawn mower and check blades	❑			
Have carpets professionally cleaned	❑			
Fertilize lawn	❑	❑	❑	❑
Have trees pruned	❑			
Clean swimming pool and filters; check water	❑ or	❑	❑	

WALL: PRIMARY PAINT / WALLPAPER

color >

brand >

finish >

type >

location of purchase >

date of work >

cost >

notes >

ATTACH SWATCH HERE

TRIM: PRIMARY PAINT

color >

brand >

finish >

type >

location of purchase >

date of work >

cost >

notes >

ATTACH SWATCH HERE

CEILING: PRIMARY PAINT

color >

brand >

finish >

type >

location of purchase >

date of work >

cost >

notes >

ATTACH SWATCH HERE

OTHER: PRIMARY PAINT

color >

brand >

finish >

type >

location of purchase >

date of work >

cost >

notes >

ATTACH SWATCH HERE

TEXTILES (CURTAINS / UPHOLSTERY)

brand >

name and style no. >

location of purchase >

work done by >

date of work >

cost >

notes >

ATTACH SWATCH HERE

TEXTILES (CURTAINS / UPHOLSTERY)

brand >

name and style no. >

location of purchase >

work done by >

date of work >

cost >

notes >

ATTACH SWATCH HERE

BLINDS / SHADES

name and style no. >

location of purchase >

work done by >

date of work >

cost >

notes >

ATTACH SWATCH HERE

OTHER FIXTURES

item >

name and style no. >

location of purchase >

cost >

notes >

GENERAL ROOM NOTES

WALL: PRIMARY PAINT / WALLPAPER

color >

brand >

finish >

type >

location of purchase >

date of work >

cost >

notes >

ATTACH SWATCH HERE

TRIM: PRIMARY PAINT

color >

brand >

finish >

type >

location of purchase >

date of work >

cost >

notes >

ATTACH SWATCH HERE

CEILING: PRIMARY PAINT

color >

brand >

finish >

type >

location of purchase >

date of work >

cost >

notes >

ATTACH SWATCH HERE

OTHER: PRIMARY PAINT

color >

brand >

finish >

type >

location of purchase >

date of work >

cost >

notes >

ATTACH SWATCH HERE

TEXTILES (CURTAINS / UPHOLSTERY)

brand >

name and style no. >

location of purchase >

work done by >

date of work >

cost >

notes >

ATTACH SWATCH HERE

TEXTILES (CURTAINS / UPHOLSTERY)

brand >

name and style no. >

location of purchase >

work done by >

date of work >

cost >

notes >

ATTACH SWATCH HERE

BLINDS / SHADES

brand >

name and style no. >

location of purchase >

work done by >

date of work >

cost >

notes >

ATTACH SWATCH HERE

OTHER FIXTURES

item >

brand >

name and style no. >

location of purchase >

cost >

notes >

GENERAL ROOM NOTES

WALL: PRIMARY PAINT / WALLPAPER

color >

brand >

finish >

type >

location of purchase >

date of work >

cost >

notes >

ATTACH SWATCH HERE

TRIM: PRIMARY PAINT

color >

brand >

finish >

type >

location of purchase >

date of work >

cost >

notes >

ATTACH SWATCH HERE

CEILING: PRIMARY PAINT

color >

brand >

finish >

type >

location of purchase >

date of work >

cost >

notes >

ATTACH SWATCH HERE

OTHER: PRIMARY PAINT

color >

brand >

finish >

type >

location of purchase >

date of work >

cost >

notes >

ATTACH SWATCH HERE

TEXTILES (CURTAINS / UPHOLSTERY)

brand >

name and style no. >

location of purchase >

work done by >

date of work >

cost >

notes >

ATTACH SWATCH HERE

TEXTILES (CURTAINS / UPHOLSTERY)

brand >

name and style no. >

location of purchase >

work done by >

date of work >

cost >

notes >

ATTACH SWATCH HERE

BLINDS / SHADES

brand >

name and style no. >

location of purchase >

work done by >

date of work >

cost >

notes >

ATTACH SWATCH HERE

OTHER FIXTURES

item >

brand >

name and style no. >

location of purchase >

cost >

notes >

GENERAL ROOM NOTES

WALL: PRIMARY PAINT / WALLPAPER

color >

brand >

finish >

type >

location of purchase >

date of work >

cost >

notes >

ATTACH SWATCH HERE

TRIM: PRIMARY PAINT

color >

brand >

finish >

type >

location of purchase >

date of work >

cost >

notes >

ATTACH SWATCH HERE

CEILING: PRIMARY PAINT

color >

brand >

finish >

type >

location of purchase >

date of work >

cost >

notes >

ATTACH SWATCH HERE

OTHER: PRIMARY PAINT

color >

brand >

finish >

type >

location of purchase >

date of work >

cost >

notes >

ATTACH SWATCH HERE

TEXTILES (CURTAINS / UPHOLSTERY)

brand >

name and style no. >

location of purchase >

work done by >

date of work >

cost >

notes >

ATTACH SWATCH HERE

TEXTILES (CURTAINS / UPHOLSTERY)

brand >

name and style no. >

location of purchase >

work done by >

date of work >

cost >

notes >

ATTACH SWATCH HERE

BLINDS / SHADES

brand >

name and style no. >

location of purchase >

work done by >

date of work >

cost >

notes >

ATTACH SWATCH HERE

OTHER FIXTURES

item >

brand >

name and style no. >

location of purchase >

cost >

notes >

GENERAL ROOM NOTES

WALL: PRIMARY PAINT / WALLPAPER

color >

brand >

finish >

type >

location of purchase >

date of work >

cost >

notes >

ATTACH SWATCH HERE

TRIM: PRIMARY PAINT

color >

brand >

finish >

type >

location of purchase >

date of work >

cost >

notes >

ATTACH SWATCH HERE

CEILING: PRIMARY PAINT

color >

brand >

finish >

type >

location of purchase >

date of work >

cost >

notes >

ATTACH SWATCH HERE

OTHER: PRIMARY PAINT

color >

brand >

finish >

type >

location of purchase >

date of work >

cost >

notes >

ATTACH SWATCH HERE

TEXTILES (CURTAINS / UPHOLSTERY)

brand >

name and style no. >

location of purchase >

work done by >

date of work >

cost >

notes >

ATTACH SWATCH HERE

TEXTILES (CURTAINS / UPHOLSTERY)

brand >

name and style no. >

location of purchase >

work done by >

date of work >

cost >

notes >

ATTACH SWATCH HERE

BLINDS / SHADES

brand >

name and style no. >

location of purchase >

work done by >

date of work >

cost >

notes >

ATTACH SWATCH HERE

OTHER FIXTURES

item >

brand >

name and style no. >

location of purchase >

cost >

notes >

GENERAL ROOM NOTES

WALL: PRIMARY PAINT / WALLPAPER

color >

brand >

finish >

type >

location of purchase >

date of work >

cost >

notes >

ATTACH SWATCH HERE

TRIM: PRIMARY PAINT

color >

brand >

finish >

type >

location of purchase >

date of work >

cost >

notes >

ATTACH SWATCH HERE

CEILING: PRIMARY PAINT

color >

brand >

finish >

type >

location of purchase >

date of work >

cost >

notes >

ATTACH SWATCH HERE

OTHER: PRIMARY PAINT

color >

brand >

finish >

type >

location of purchase >

date of work >

cost >

notes >

ATTACH SWATCH HERE

TEXTILES (CURTAINS / UPHOLSTERY)

brand >

name and style no. >

location of purchase >

work done by >

date of work >

cost >

notes >

ATTACH SWATCH HERE

TEXTILES (CURTAINS / UPHOLSTERY)

brand >

name and style no. >

location of purchase >

work done by >

date of work >

cost >

notes >

ATTACH SWATCH HERE

BLINDS / SHADES

brand >

name and style no. >

location of purchase >

work done by >

date of work >

cost >

notes >

ATTACH SWATCH HERE

OTHER FIXTURES

item >

brand >

name and style no. >

location of purchase >

cost >

notes >

GENERAL ROOM NOTES

WALL: PRIMARY PAINT / WALLPAPER

color >

brand >

finish >

type >

location of purchase >

date of work >

cost >

notes >

ATTACH SWATCH HERE

TRIM: PRIMARY PAINT

color >

brand >

finish >

type >

location of purchase >

date of work >

cost >

notes >

ATTACH SWATCH HERE

CEILING: PRIMARY PAINT

color >

brand >

finish >

type >

location of purchase >

date of work >

cost >

notes >

ATTACH SWATCH HERE

OTHER: PRIMARY PAINT

color >

brand >

finish >

type >

location of purchase >

date of work >

cost >

notes >

ATTACH SWATCH HERE

TEXTILES (CURTAINS / UPHOLSTERY)

brand >

name and style no. >

location of purchase >

work done by >

date of work >

cost >

notes >

ATTACH SWATCH HERE

TEXTILES (CURTAINS / UPHOLSTERY)

brand >

name and style no. >

location of purchase >

work done by >

date of work >

cost >

notes >

ATTACH SWATCH HERE

BLINDS / SHADES

brand >

name and style no. >

location of purchase >

work done by >

date of work >

cost >

notes >

ATTACH SWATCH HERE

OTHER FIXTURES

item >

brand >

name and style no. >

location of purchase >

cost >

notes >

GENERAL ROOM NOTES

WALL: PRIMARY PAINT / WALLPAPER

color >

brand >

finish >

type >

location of purchase >

date of work >

cost >

notes >

ATTACH SWATCH HERE

TRIM: PRIMARY PAINT

color >

brand >

finish >

type >

location of purchase >

date of work >

cost >

notes >

ATTACH SWATCH HERE

CEILING: PRIMARY PAINT

color >

brand >

finish >

type >

location of purchase >

date of work >

cost >

notes >

ATTACH SWATCH HERE

OTHER: PRIMARY PAINT

color >

brand >

finish >

type >

location of purchase >

date of work >

cost >

notes >

ATTACH SWATCH HERE

TEXTILES (CURTAINS / UPHOLSTERY)

brand >

name and style no. >

location of purchase >

work done by >

date of work >

cost >

notes >

ATTACH SWATCH HERE

TEXTILES (CURTAINS / UPHOLSTERY)

brand >

name and style no. >

location of purchase >

work done by >

date of work >

cost >

notes >

ATTACH SWATCH HERE

BLINDS / SHADES

brand >

name and style no. >

location of purchase >

work done by >

date of work >

cost >

notes >

ATTACH SWATCH HERE

OTHER FIXTURES

item >

brand >

name and style no. >

location of purchase >

cost >

notes >

GENERAL ROOM NOTES

WALL: PRIMARY PAINT / WALLPAPER

color >

brand >

finish >

type >

location of purchase >

date of work >

cost >

notes >

ATTACH SWATCH HERE

TRIM: PRIMARY PAINT

color >

brand >

finish >

type >

location of purchase >

date of work >

cost >

notes >

ATTACH SWATCH HERE

CEILING: PRIMARY PAINT

color >

brand >

finish >

type >

location of purchase >

date of work >

cost >

notes >

ATTACH SWATCH HERE

OTHER: PRIMARY PAINT

color >

brand >

finish >

type >

location of purchase >

date of work >

cost >

notes >

ATTACH SWATCH HERE

TEXTILES (CURTAINS / UPHOLSTERY)

brand >

name and style no. >

location of purchase >

work done by >

date of work >

cost >

notes >

ATTACH SWATCH HERE

TEXTILES (CURTAINS / UPHOLSTERY)

brand >

name and style no. >

location of purchase >

work done by >

date of work >

cost >

notes >

ATTACH SWATCH HERE

BLINDS / SHADES

brand >

name and style no. >

location of purchase >

work done by >

date of work >

cost >

notes >

ATTACH SWATCH HERE

OTHER FIXTURES

item >

brand >

name and style no. >

location of purchase >

cost >

notes >

GENERAL ROOM NOTES

WALL: PRIMARY PAINT / WALLPAPER

color >

brand >

finish >

type >

location of purchase >

date of work >

cost >

notes >

ATTACH SWATCH HERE

TRIM: PRIMARY PAINT

color >

brand >

finish >

type >

location of purchase >

date of work >

cost >

notes >

ATTACH SWATCH HERE

CEILING: PRIMARY PAINT

color >

brand >

finish >

type >

location of purchase >

date of work >

cost >

notes >

ATTACH SWATCH HERE

OTHER: PRIMARY PAINT

color >

brand >

finish >

type >

location of purchase >

date of work >

cost >

notes >

ATTACH SWATCH HERE

TEXTILES (CURTAINS / UPHOLSTERY)

brand >

name and style no. >

location of purchase >

work done by >

date of work >

cost >

notes >

ATTACH SWATCH HERE

TEXTILES (CURTAINS / UPHOLSTERY)

brand >

name and style no. >

location of purchase >

work done by >

date of work >

cost >

notes >

ATTACH SWATCH HERE

BLINDS / SHADES

brand >

name and style no. >

location of purchase >

work done by >

date of work >

cost >

notes >

ATTACH SWATCH HERE

OTHER FIXTURES

item >

brand >

name and style no. >

location of purchase >

cost >

notes >

GENERAL ROOM NOTES

WALL: PRIMARY PAINT / WALLPAPER

color >

brand >

finish >

type >

location of purchase >

date of work >

cost >

notes >

ATTACH SWATCH HERE

TRIM: PRIMARY PAINT

color >

brand >

finish >

type >

location of purchase >

date of work >

cost >

notes >

ATTACH SWATCH HERE

CEILING: PRIMARY PAINT

color >

brand >

finish >

type >

location of purchase >

date of work >

cost >

notes >

ATTACH SWATCH HERE

OTHER: PRIMARY PAINT

color >

brand >

finish >

type >

location of purchase >

date of work >

cost >

notes >

ATTACH SWATCH HERE

TEXTILES (CURTAINS / UPHOLSTERY)

brand >

name and style no. >

location of purchase >

work done by >

date of work >

cost >

notes >

ATTACH SWATCH HERE

TEXTILES (CURTAINS / UPHOLSTERY)

brand >

name and style no. >

location of purchase >

work done by >

date of work >

cost >

notes >

ATTACH SWATCH HERE

BLINDS / SHADES

brand >

name and style no. >

location of purchase >

work done by >

date of work >

cost >

notes >

ATTACH SWATCH HERE

OTHER FIXTURES

item >

brand >

name and style no. >

location of purchase >

cost >

notes >

GENERAL ROOM NOTES

WALL: PRIMARY PAINT / WALLPAPER

color >

brand >

finish >

type >

location of purchase >

date of work >

cost >

notes >

ATTACH SWATCH HERE

TRIM: PRIMARY PAINT

color >

brand >

finish >

type >

location of purchase >

date of work >

cost >

notes >

ATTACH SWATCH HERE

CEILING: PRIMARY PAINT

color >

brand >

finish >

type >

location of purchase >

date of work >

cost >

notes >

ATTACH SWATCH HERE

OTHER: PRIMARY PAINT

color >

brand >

finish >

type >

location of purchase >

date of work >

cost >

notes >

ATTACH SWATCH HERE

TEXTILES (CURTAINS / UPHOLSTERY)

brand >

name and style no. >

location of purchase >

work done by >

date of work >

cost >

notes >

ATTACH SWATCH HERE

TEXTILES (CURTAINS / UPHOLSTERY)

brand >

name and style no. >

location of purchase >

work done by >

date of work >

cost >

notes >

ATTACH SWATCH HERE

BLINDS / SHADES

brand >

name and style no. >

location of purchase >

work done by >

date of work >

cost >

notes >

ATTACH SWATCH HERE

OTHER FIXTURES

item >

brand >

name and style no. >

location of purchase >

cost >

notes >

GENERAL ROOM NOTES

WALL: PRIMARY PAINT / WALLPAPER

color >

brand >

finish >

type >

location of purchase >

date of work >

cost >

notes >

ATTACH SWATCH HERE

TRIM: PRIMARY PAINT

color >

brand >

finish >

type >

location of purchase >

date of work >

cost >

notes >

ATTACH SWATCH HERE

CEILING: PRIMARY PAINT

color >

brand >

finish >

type >

location of purchase >

date of work >

cost >

notes >

ATTACH SWATCH HERE

OTHER: PRIMARY PAINT

color >

brand >

finish >

type >

location of purchase >

date of work >

cost >

notes >

ATTACH SWATCH HERE

TEXTILES (CURTAINS / UPHOLSTERY)

brand >

name and style no. >

location of purchase >

work done by >

date of work >

cost >

notes >

ATTACH SWATCH HERE

TEXTILES (CURTAINS / UPHOLSTERY)

brand >

name and style no. >

location of purchase >

work done by >

date of work >

cost >

notes >

ATTACH SWATCH HERE

BLINDS / SHADES

brand >

name and style no. >

location of purchase >

work done by >

date of work >

cost >

notes >

ATTACH SWATCH HERE

OTHER FIXTURES

item >

brand >

name and style no. >

location of purchase >

cost >

notes >

GENERAL ROOM NOTES

WALL: PRIMARY PAINT / WALLPAPER

color >

brand >

finish >

type >

location of purchase >

date of work >

cost >

notes >

ATTACH SWATCH HERE

TRIM: PRIMARY PAINT

color >

brand >

finish >

type >

location of purchase >

date of work >

cost >

notes >

ATTACH SWATCH HERE

CEILING: PRIMARY PAINT

color >

brand >

finish >

type >

location of purchase >

date of work >

cost >

notes >

ATTACH SWATCH HERE

OTHER: PRIMARY PAINT

color >

brand >

finish >

type >

location of purchase >

date of work >

cost >

notes >

ATTACH SWATCH HERE

TEXTILES (CURTAINS / UPHOLSTERY)

brand >

name and style no. >

location of purchase >

work done by >

date of work >

cost >

notes >

ATTACH SWATCH HERE

TEXTILES (CURTAINS / UPHOLSTERY)

brand >

name and style no. >

location of purchase >

work done by >

date of work >

cost >

notes >

ATTACH SWATCH HERE

BLINDS / SHADES

brand >

name and style no. >

location of purchase >

work done by >

date of work >

cost >

notes >

ATTACH SWATCH HERE

OTHER FIXTURES

item >

brand >

name and style no. >

location of purchase >

cost >

notes >

GENERAL ROOM NOTES

flooring: hardwood

AREA OF HOUSE >

wood type >

board width >

stain >

finish >

date of installation >

cost >

notes on maintenance >

refinishing

date >

work done by >

cost >

date >

work done by >

cost >

date >

work done by >

cost >

AREA OF HOUSE >

wood type >

board width >

stain >

finish >

date of installation >

cost >

notes on maintenance >

refinishing

date >

work done by >

cost >

date >

work done by >

cost >

date >

work done by >

cost >

MAINTENANCE TIPS: Use felt or rubber glides under all movable furniture to protect the floor surface from scrapes. Never drag anything heavy across your wood floors. Be sure to mop up any drips or spills quickly, even water, as moisture left on hardwood floors will damage the finish. Frequent vacuuming of high-traffic areas will preserve the finish longer.

flooring: carpeting

AREA OF HOUSE >

brand >

color and style no. >

location of purchase >

installed by >

date of installation >

cost >

notes on maintenance >

carpet cleaning

date >

work done by >

cost >

date >

work done by >

cost >

date >

work done by >

cost >

AREA OF HOUSE >

brand >

color and style no. >

location of purchase >

installed by >

date of installation >

cost >

notes on maintenance >

MAINTENANCE TIPS: It is important to have carpets professionally cleaned, but do not be overeager, because the more you get your carpets cleaned, the more you will have to get them cleaned again. Steam-cleaning loosens the coils of the carpet fibers and allows dirt to accumulate more quickly than before. The best way to maintain carpets is not to wear shoes on them and to vacuum regularly. Another option is to place large, heavy-duty doormats at each outside entrance. Try to do all professional cleaning during the summer, when you can ventilate adequately afterward.

carpet cleaning

date >

work done by >

cost >

date >

work done by >

cost >

flooring: carpeting

AREA OF HOUSE >

brand >

color and style no. >

location of purchase >

installed by >

date of installation >

cost >

notes on maintenance >

carpet cleaning

date >

work done by >

cost >

date >

work done by >

cost >

date >

work done by >

cost >

flooring: linoleum / tile / other

ROOM >

brand >

color and style no. >

location of purchase >

installed by >

date of installation >

cost >

notes on maintenance >

ROOM >

brand >

color and style no. >

location of purchase >

installed by >

date of installation >

cost >

notes on maintenance >

ROOM >

brand >

color and style no. >

location of purchase >

installed by >

date of installation >

cost >

notes on maintenance >

WASHING MACHINE

brand >

model >

location of purchase >

date of purchase >

cost >

duration of warranty >

> **MAINTENANCE TIPS:** Consider buying stainless-steel braided hoses to replace the rubber pipes in your washing machine, as rubber corrodes over time and can eventually crack and cause flooding.

repairs / maintenance

date >

type of work >

repair company >

cost >

notes >

date >

type of work >

repair company >

cost >

notes >

DRYER

brand >

model >

location of purchase >

date of purchase >

cost >

duration of warranty >

> **MAINTENANCE TIPS:** Clean out vents and ducts once a year. Always remove lint from the filter before every load.

repairs / maintenance

date >

type of work >

repair company >

cost >

notes >

date >

type of work >

repair company >

cost >

notes >

REFRIGERATOR

brand >

model >

location of purchase >

date of purchase >

cost >

duration of warranty >

MAINTENANCE TIPS: Vacuum out the coils and vents below or behind your refrigerator at least twice a year to ensure maximum efficiency (especially if you have pets whose hair is likely to accumulate underneath). If you have an ice maker, consider replacing its rubber hose with a stainless-steel braided hose, which will not corrode or crack. Clean out the interior at least once every six months.

repairs / maintenance

date >

type of work >

repair company >

cost >

notes >

date >

type of work >

repair company >

cost >

notes >

DISHWASHER

brand >

model >

location of purchase >

date of purchase >

cost >

duration of warranty >

MAINTENANCE TIPS: Consider replacing rubber hose with a stainless-steel braided hose. Avoid using too much dish detergent. If you see evidence of discoloration on your dishes, buy a rust solution at your local appliance store, place a capful in the soap basin, and run it without any dishes. This should remove any residue.

repairs / maintenance

date >

type of work >

repair company >

cost >

notes >

date >

type of work >

repair company >

cost >

notes >

OVEN / STOVE / MICROWAVE

brand >

model >

location of purchase >

date of purchase >

cost >

duration of warranty >

MAINTENANCE TIPS: Clean the fan or venting system at least twice a year, as grease buildup can cause a fire.

repairs / maintenance

date >

type of work >

repair company >

cost >

notes >

date >

type of work >

repair company >

cost >

notes >

WATER HEATER

brand >

model >

location of purchase >

date of purchase >

cost >

duration of warranty >

MAINTENANCE TIPS: Have the water heater inspected once a year. Wrap it in an insulation blanket to save energy. If you live in an area prone to earthquakes, strap the heater down.

repairs / maintenance

date >

type of work >

repair company >

cost >

notes >

date >

type of work >

repair company >

cost >

notes >

WOOD STOVE / FIREPLACE

brand >

model >

location of purchase >

date of purchase >

cost >

duration of warranty >

MAINTENANCE TIPS: Be sure to have your chimney cleaned and inspected once a year.

professional cleaning / maintenance

date >

type of work >

cleaning company >

cost >

notes >

date >

type of work >

cleaning company >

cost >

notes >

LAWN MOWER

brand >

model >

location of purchase >

date of purchase >

cost >

duration of warranty >

MAINTENANCE TIPS: Change the oil at least once a year. Check the blades and replace when necessary.

repairs / maintenance

date >

type of work >

repair company >

cost >

notes >

date >

type of work >

repair company >

cost >

notes >

appliances and equipment

VACUUM CLEANER

brand >

model >

location of purchase >

date of purchase >

cost >

duration of warranty >

MAINTENANCE TIPS: Remember to change vacuum bags regularly and remove any hair or other items stuck in the components.

repairs / maintenance

date >

type of work >

repair company >

cost >

notes >

date >

type of work >

repair company >

cost >

notes >

pest control

date >

what was done >

pest control company >

cost >

notes >

date >

what was done >

pest control company >

cost >

notes >

date >

what was done >

pest control company >

cost >

notes >

date >

what was done >

pest control company >

cost >

notes >

exterior: general structure (paint / foundation / etc.)

PRIMARY PAINT / SHINGLE / WOOD / ETC.

color/stain >

brand/style >

finish >

type >

location of purchase >

date of work >

cost >

duration of warranty (if applicable) >

ATTACH SWATCH HERE

TRIM

color/stain >

brand/style >

finish >

type >

location of purchase >

date of work >

cost >

duration of warranty (if applicable) >

ATTACH SWATCH HERE

repairs / maintenance

date >

type of work >

repair company >

cost >

notes >

date >

type of work >

repair company >

cost >

notes >

date >

type of work >

repair company >

cost >

notes >

MAINTENANCE TIPS: Be cautious when planting vines or other creepers along the side of your house. Over time, popular plants such as ivy and bougainvillea can do serious damage to its structural integrity. Always use trellises to keep the plants away from the exterior walls.

Check for cracks in foundation annually and for proper drainage around the house.

yard / garden

date >

work done by >

type of work >

cost >

notes >

date >

work done by >

type of work >

cost >

notes >

date >

work done by >

type of work >

cost >

notes >

date >

work done by >

type of work >

cost >

notes >

date >

work done by >

type of work >

cost >

notes >

date >

work done by >

type of work >

cost >

notes >

date >

work done by >

type of work >

cost >

notes >

date >

work done by >

type of work >

cost >

notes >

date >

work done by >

type of work >

cost >

notes >

MAINTENANCE TIPS: Get fruit trees pruned annually. Fertilize the lawn once every three months. Inspect and winterize irrigation system. Remove weeds. Weeding every two to three weeks takes less time and effort in the long run than waiting until the area is overgrown.

garage and driveway

date > _____

type of work > _____

work done by > _____

cost > _____

notes > _____

date > _____

type of work > _____

work done by > _____

cost > _____

notes > _____

MAINTENANCE TIPS: An asphalt driveway requires little to no maintenance, but keep an eye on it to make sure there are no cracks, and have it resurfaced if necessary. If you have a gravel driveway, you may find you need a fresh supply of gravel every few years. A properly functioning automatic garage door opener shouldn't require any maintenance, but if you are having one installed, make a note of who did the work here in case you have any trouble with it later on.

gravel driveways

type of gravel > _____

location of purchase > _____

date > _____

cost > _____

notes > _____

porch / deck / patio / terrace

PRIMARY PAINT / STAIN / OIL

color/stain > _____

brand/style > _____

finish > _____

type > _____

location of purchase > _____

date of work > _____

cost > _____

notes > _____

ATTACH SWATCH HERE

repairs / maintenance

date > _____

type of work > _____

repair company > _____

cost > _____

notes > _____

date > _____

type of work > _____

repair company > _____

cost > _____

notes > _____

MAINTENANCE TIPS: Inspect annually for signs of rot or mildew. Keep clean. Reapply a preservative seal if you see signs of deterioration.

roof

PRIMARY MATERIAL

color/stain >

brand/style >

finish >

type >

location of purchase >

date of work >

cost >

duration of warranty (if applicable) >

notes >

MAINTENANCE TIPS: Inspect annually. Keep clean. Do not let moss accumulate. If you have an attic, check for leaks from inside when the rainy season starts.

repairs / maintenance

date >

type of work >

repair company >

cost >

notes >

date >

type of work >

repair company >

cost >

notes >

fence

PRIMARY PAINT / STAIN / OIL

color/stain >

brand/style >

finish >

type >

location of purchase >

date of work >

cost >

notes >

ATTACH SWATCH HERE

repairs / maintenance

date >

type of work >

repair company >

cost >

notes >

date >

type of work >

repair company >

cost >

notes >

windows and glass

date >

type of work >

work done by >

cost >

notes >

date >

type of work >

work done by >

cost >

notes >

date >

type of work >

work done by >

cost >

notes >

MAINTENANCE TIPS: Check to make sure that window seals are in good condition. It's a good idea to do this in the fall before you turn on the heat for the winter season to ensure that heat isn't escaping through cracks.

gutters and downspouts

date >

type of work >

work done by >

cost >

notes >

date >

type of work >

work done by >

cost >

notes >

date >

type of work >

work done by >

cost >

notes >

date >

type of work >

work done by >

cost >

notes >

date >

type of work >

work done by >

cost >

notes >

MAINTENANCE TIPS: Remove debris at least once a year (in the fall is best). Consider purchasing gutter guards to help drainage.

systems

HEATING AND COOLING SYSTEM

brand >

model >

location of purchase >

date of purchase >

cost >

duration of warranty >

notes >

> **MAINTENANCE TIPS**: Remember to clean or replace the filters every three months. Have the furnace inspected annually.

repairs / maintenance

date >

type of work >

repair company >

cost >

notes >

date >

type of work >

repair company >

cost >

notes >

ELECTRICAL SYSTEM

date > March 5, 2008

type of work > General

repair company > Joe MANchester Elec

cost >

notes > Kitchen overhead (counter) 12 volt MR 16/50 Watt

date >

type of work >

repair company >

cost >

notes >

date >

type of work >

repair company >

cost >

notes >

date >

type of work >

repair company >

cost >

notes >

PLUMBING

date >

type of work >

repair company >

cost >

notes >

date >

type of work >

repair company >

cost >

notes >

date >

type of work >

repair company >

cost >

notes >

date >

type of work >

repair company >

cost >

notes >

SEPTIC TANK

date >

type of work >

repair company >

cost >

notes >

date >

type of work >

repair company >

cost >

notes >

MAINTENANCE TIPS: The level should be checked annually and pumped every five years or so.

date >

type of work >

repair company >

cost >

notes >

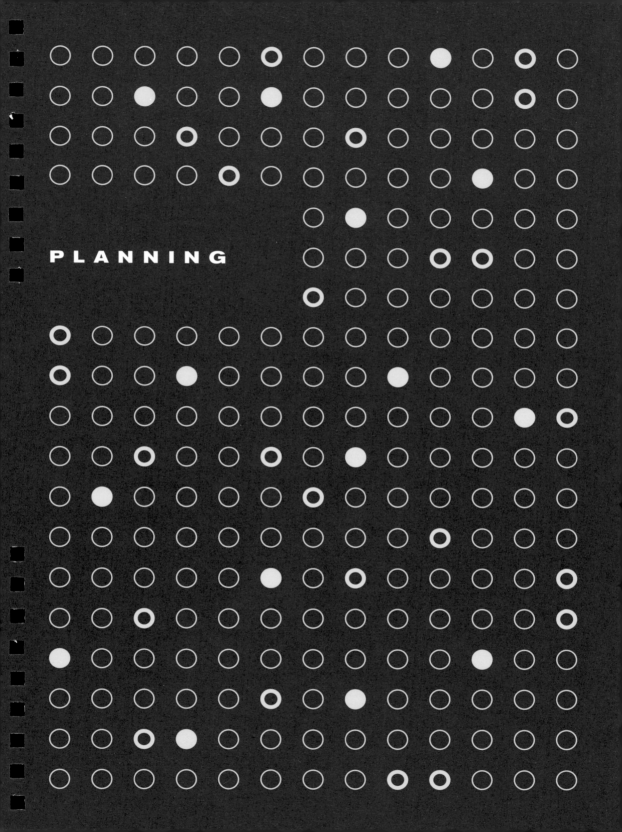

PLANNING

This section provides a space for you to keep track of your ideas as you think about decorating your home. Although you may not be able to make any major changes right away, it's worth taking note of things you see that appeal to you. Have fun with this: paste in clippings of rooms that you like, take note of stores that suit your style, and mark down homes or rooms that might provide inspiration in the future. If you are struck by the general look of a room and want to remember it, paste a picture of it in here for future reference. If a friend just put in built-in bookshelves and you like the way the work was done, this is the place to jot down the name of the builder. When a colleague mentions a great online source for lighting fixtures, write it down here. If a neighbor got especially great service or a great deal somewhere, make a note of those places and people. Collect potentially useful business cards in the plastic sleeves of this record book. Sketch out your ideas as you think about how to adapt elements from other places into your own home. You will end up with a highly customized home design directory and scrapbook for inspiration.

Keep in mind that it is often easier to get inspiration through example than in the abstract. Many of us have trouble imagining all the possibilities for our homes and don't know where to look. Your local library is a great place to begin. It probably has several shelves devoted to home decor and improvement, which can give you a preliminary sense of your options. The library is also a good place to look through back issues of decor magazines — especially if there's a specific look you have in mind and want to learn more about it. Check out open houses and home tours. Think of places that have made you feel comfortable and at home. Supply-store displays can give you some ideas if you're trying to figure out what various materials look like in a kitchen or bathroom. Hotels can be great sources of inspiration for bathroom fixtures, and keep an eye out in restaurants, which often have interesting wall coverings and lighting fixtures. Keep an eye out at friends' houses, too. Look at the room backgrounds in lifestyle and furniture catalogs and brochures, and keep track of it all here.

As you develop your eye for home decor, try to break down the various elements of those places you admired: Was it the curtains that made them so cozy? The bookshelves that gave them such character? The vintage rocking chair that was so inviting? Over time, you will get a better sense of your own style. When you survey a room, consider how the following elements influence it: lighting (natural light versus overhead and lamp-lit), furnishings, floor surfaces, textiles, moldings, framing, wainscoting, wallpaper, window coverings, fixtures, and shelving. As you think about how to best use the space in your own rooms, remember to consider things such as unity of style, long-term satisfaction, scale, practicality, mobility, purpose, storage needs, and views. Although it may be difficult at first to assess what makes a room "work," you can train your eye to focus on the features that endow it with a given feel.

Your home is the ultimate expression of yourself. Use your imagination here. Be creative. This is the place to set restraint aside and dream. Although you may not be able to achieve exactly what you want right away, it is worthwhile to think about what you really want from your home over the long term. Think about how to give it flair and make it yours.

Expenses 2004

memorable rooms and features

notable features >

notes >

Item	Where Purchased	Cost
1. Oriental Rug	Landry/Arcari	6,915.00
2. "	"	3,365.00

PICTURES / SKETCHES

memorable rooms and features

notable features >

notes >

PICTURES / SKETCHES

memorable rooms and features

notable features >

notes >

PICTURES / SKETCHES

memorable rooms and features

notable features >

notes >

PICTURES / SKETCHES

memorable rooms and features

notable features >

notes >

PICTURES / SKETCHES

memorable rooms and features

notable features >

notes >

PICTURES / SKETCHES

sources

STORE >

address >

phone >

web site >

specialty >

items of interest >

notes >

STORE >

address >

phone >

web site >

specialty >

items of interest >

notes >

STORE >

address >

phone >

web site >

specialty >

items of interest >

notes >

STORE >

address >

phone >

web site >

specialty >

items of interest >

notes >

STORE >

address >

phone >

web site >

specialty >

items of interest >

notes >

STORE >

address >

phone >

web site >

specialty >

items of interest >

notes >

sources

STORE >

address >

phone >

web site >

specialty >

items of interest >

notes >

STORE >

address >

phone >

web site >

specialty >

items of interest >

notes >

STORE >

address >

phone >

web site >

specialty >

items of interest >

notes >

STORE >

address >

phone >

web site >

specialty >

items of interest >

notes >

STORE >

address >

phone >

web site >

specialty >

items of interest >

notes >

STORE >

address >

phone >

web site >

specialty >

items of interest >

notes >

sources

STORE >

address >

phone >

web site >

specialty >

items of interest >

notes >

STORE >

address >

phone >

web site >

specialty >

items of interest >

notes >

STORE >

address >

phone >

web site >

specialty >

items of interest >

notes >

STORE >

address >

phone >

web site >

specialty >

items of interest >

notes >

STORE >

address >

phone >

web site >

specialty >

items of interest >

notes >

STORE >

address >

phone >

web site >

specialty >

items of interest >

notes >

sources

STORE >

address >

phone >

web site >

specialty >

items of interest >

notes >

STORE >

address >

phone >

web site >

specialty >

items of interest >

notes >

STORE >

address >

phone >

web site >

specialty >

items of interest >

notes >

STORE >

address >

phone >

web site >

specialty >

items of interest >

notes >

STORE >

address >

phone >

web site >

specialty >

items of interest >

notes >

STORE >

address >

phone >

web site >

specialty >

items of interest >

notes >

The Resources and Inspiration section is a place for you to dream. This section will help you figure out how to achieve those dreams. You may think of a thousand improvements and repairs, large and small, that you'd like to make in your home. "Wouldn't it be nice...to have a bigger closet, built-in bookshelves, a claw-foot tub, a sprinkler system, a gas stove?" Although that can be fun and exciting, it also can be overwhelming. Where to begin?

It is all too easy to tackle small projects in a piecemeal fashion and end up with no money for the bigger, more vital jobs. As you consider what projects will best enhance your life, you must remember to set aside time and money for routine maintenance. Often the costs of such maintenance are low, but you need to balance them with the more cosmetically satisfying, quality-of-life-enhancing projects. This section will help you sort out how to take action in such a way that you won't land in massive debt or be left stranded with delayed repairs and unfinished jobs when the seasonal rains set in.

As you get to know your house, jot down changes you'd like to make. Once you have a sense of how you use your home day-to-day and what it's like to live there through different seasons, review your list. Consider the following lifestyle questions to get started:

- In which rooms do you spend the most time?
- Do you cook often? Does your current kitchen keep you from cooking more often?
- Do you entertain frequently? Is your current setup adequate for holidays and other social activities?
- Do you like to garden? Are you making the most of your outdoor area?
- Do you have enough space for the things you like to do? (Hobbies, projects, work at home, etc?)
- Is your storage space sufficient, or are you spilling out of your closets?
- Do you plan to have kids soon, or do you already? Do you want a kid-friendly house?

- Is saving money your top priority?
- How long do you plan to stay in this house?
- Which chores take you the most time? Is there a way to cut down on the work with an automated system, such as an automatic sprinkler, a self-propelled lawn mower, or a washing machine?
- Are there energy-saving measures you should consider?
- Do you have or want pets?
- Are there safety precautions that you need to implement? (Remove dead trees, take earthquake safety measures?)

As you tackle the question of what should come first, remember to think ahead—further ahead than you might be used to. Think long and hard about how you use your space and what will affect the quality of your daily life, and try to focus on projects that will enhance your day-to-day routine: Is watering the lawn taking up all your spare time? Then maybe an irrigation system is more important than built-in speakers. Is installing a money-saving auto-thermostat going to be your most valuable accomplishment this year?

Another factor to consider is how to increase the value of your investment. If you think you might sell your home in the next few years, prioritize changes that will increase the property value, as some home decor additions add more value than others. It's worth consulting a real estate agent for tips and suggestions if you are unsure about what will yield the greater return later on. Given the choice between putting in wood floors and improving your landscaping, the floors will add more value. Think about whether you want to invest in improvements you can take with you (furniture, a chandelier, rugs) or ones that will pay off when you sell. Finally, remember that it is likely worthwhile to wait longer to do a project, so that you can do it right, because you may come to regret the cheap, quick-fix solutions when it comes time to sell.

Depending on the size of your yard, landscaping can take up a great deal of time. It's a great pastime if you love gardening, but be careful about how much you decide to take on. Your options vary; if you want a relatively low-maintenance yard, choose shrubs and trees accordingly. Try to resist falling in love with high-maintenance annuals if you don't have the time or inclination to water, fertilize, weed, and prune. If you are ready to commit time and money to your outdoor space, consider professional advice from a landscaper. A yard is just like a room in your home: It is best not to embark on changes in a piecemeal fashion, but to conceive a plan in its entirety and then take it step by step.

Often, the single biggest factor in determining what will get done is how much money you have to throw at the problem. Early on, as you recover from the weighty down payment and closing costs, you will likely need to focus on rebuilding a cushion for emergencies, because as a homeowner, you must always be prepared for the unexpected. Whatever your means, after replenishing your savings, you should try to come up with an annual house budget. This can be difficult at first, but will give you more flexibility down the road when you are deciding what gets done.

As you compare prices and figure out how to save money, remember to think long term. When it comes to buying items for your home—appliances, tools, furniture, floor coverings, or anything else—longevity becomes a central part of the equation. Whenever possible, buy quality, which will prove its worth 10 and 20 years later. Is this the couch you'll want in 20 years, or will you want to upgrade in five years? Will I be happy using this stove for 40 years? High-quality paint will coat better, last longer, chip less, and may require fewer layers, so it will likely end up saving you money in the long run. The higher-quality carpet will show less wear and tear in 10 years than the cheaper alternative. It may take longer to buy better, but you will enjoy it more, and also benefit when it comes time to sell. It can be expensive to buy top-of-the-line stuff, so keep an eye out for floor models that go on sale from time to time, as well as offerings through outlets, credit card deals, rebate deals, and seasonal sales. Check out the *Consumer Reports* analyses when you're trying to figure out what will serve you best.

With regard to appliances, it pays to shop around. Don't only check the big chains — sometimes a local retailer will give better deals. If you are doing a major remodel, ask for a bid for an entire group of appliances, as prices are negotiable on higher-end items, especially when you're dealing with local merchants. Energy-efficient appliances often pay for themselves in energy savings over a relatively short time, so don't balk at a higher price. Again, quality will serve you well over time: all appliances will generally work well in the first few years, but you will be able to tell the difference 10 years down the road. Finally, do remember that repair and parts for foreign appliances often cost more (and it may take longer to get them).

If saving money is the priority, limit yourself to goals that will ultimately save you money. If money is tight, then preventive maintenance is all the more vital: You simply cannot afford to ignore basic home care. In addition to setting aside money for basic home maintenance, you may want to consider implementing some of the energy-saving measures that follow. Although they lack the instant gratification of high-visibility cosmetic improvements, you will reap the benefits when the midwinter energy bill arrives. Check your energy company's Web site for additional suggestions.

- Installing motion-detecting outdoor lights
- Buying high-efficiency appliances
- Installing double-paned windows
- Resealing windows and doors
- Hanging lined curtains
- Installing an auto-thermostat
- Using a wood stove
- Insulating pipes

If you can afford it, you may want to consider bringing an architect in to give you suggestions. It's hard to visualize the full extent of the possibilities for your home if you have little experience thinking spatially. Create a master plan. If it's too overwhelming to come up with a long-term plan, begin with a two-to-three-year plan. Either way, sit down once a year and plan out what you intend to do that year and when. The following charts will help you think about how to balance your needs against timing and financial considerations. You may want to modify them to suit your specific needs, but this general form will give you a sense of how to break down all the pieces and look at the big picture.

This worksheet can help you figure out what needs to get done, how much money to set aside for it, and how to spread out the expenses over the course of the year. It can also serve as a good reminder of maintenance that you might otherwise forget or delay.

YEAR: 1

WINTER PROJECT	BUDGET	NOTES / REASONS
insulate attic	$1,000	

SPRING PROJECT	BUDGET	NOTES / REASONS
have sick tree removed	$1,000	safety precaution, top priority
have a/c system inspected	$100	

SUMMER PROJECT	BUDGET	NOTES / REASONS
have carpets cleaned	$200	after puppy is trained
stain shingles	$500	

FALL PROJECT	BUDGET	NOTES / REASONS
have furnace inspected	$100	
have chimney cleaned	$100	

TOTAL ESTIMATE: $3,000

PRIORITIES

trees (safety) and attic (need space for eventual playroom)

GENERAL NOTES

shingles could be deferred to next year if need be

goal planning

WINTER PROJECT

BUDGET

NOTES / REASONS

SPRING PROJECT

BUDGET

NOTES / REASONS

SUMMER PROJECT

BUDGET

NOTES / REASONS

FALL PROJECT

BUDGET

NOTES / REASONS

TOTAL ESTIMATE:

PRIORITIES

GENERAL NOTES

goal planning

WINTER PROJECT	BUDGET	NOTES / REASONS

SPRING PROJECT	BUDGET	NOTES / REASONS

SUMMER PROJECT	BUDGET	NOTES / REASONS

FALL PROJECT	BUDGET	NOTES / REASONS

TOTAL ESTIMATE:

PRIORITIES

GENERAL NOTES

goal planning

WINTER PROJECT	BUDGET	NOTES / REASONS

SPRING PROJECT	BUDGET	NOTES / REASONS

SUMMER PROJECT	BUDGET	NOTES / REASONS

FALL PROJECT	BUDGET	NOTES / REASONS

TOTAL ESTIMATE:

PRIORITIES

GENERAL NOTES

goal planning

WINTER PROJECT	BUDGET	NOTES / REASONS

SPRING PROJECT	BUDGET	NOTES / REASONS

SUMMER PROJECT	BUDGET	NOTES / REASONS

FALL PROJECT	BUDGET	NOTES / REASONS

TOTAL ESTIMATE:

PRIORITIES

GENERAL NOTES

goal planning

WINTER PROJECT	BUDGET	NOTES / REASONS

SPRING PROJECT	BUDGET	NOTES / REASONS

SUMMER PROJECT	BUDGET	NOTES / REASONS

FALL PROJECT	BUDGET	NOTES / REASONS

TOTAL ESTIMATE:

PRIORITIES

GENERAL NOTES

goal planning

WINTER PROJECT	BUDGET	NOTES / REASONS

SPRING PROJECT	BUDGET	NOTES / REASONS

SUMMER PROJECT	BUDGET	NOTES / REASONS

FALL PROJECT	BUDGET	NOTES / REASONS

TOTAL ESTIMATE:

PRIORITIES

GENERAL NOTES

If you are reading this section, then you are probably ready to take action. Depending on the scale of the project and your home-improvement skills, you can either hire a professional or do it yourself. Worksheets and tips for each scenario follow.

HIRING A PROFESSIONAL > When you are trying to find names of whom to contact, try the following: the Yellow Pages, neighbors, friends, colleagues, family, building-supply companies, other contractors, the Internet (handymanonline.com, for instance), hardware stores, real estate agents, architects, the store where you bought the materials. Whenever possible, get names from a source you know and trust.

Be sure to secure the proper permits from your local Planning and Zoning Commission, and obtain a plan of the house and any septic system and drain field from your local county before proceeding with any major changes.

Plan ahead, as contractors get busy, especially for seasonal work. Do not embark on any project with too tight a deadline (e.g., new baby due two weeks after completion), because chances are good that the project will take longer than you think. Don't cut corners, have the job finished badly, or add stress to the process with a looming deadline. Assume it will take longer than planned.

It is also safest to assume from the beginning that the project will go over budget, especially if it is a major remodel or addition. Leave a financial cushion for the unexpected, as mistakes do happen. Also, remember that contractors can bid only on what they can see, so if dry rot or other surprises are lurking beneath the surface, the contract will have to be modified. Don't add to the stress of not being able to get the job finished as soon as you wanted it, or exactly as you first planned it; give yourself the leeway to make changes along the way.

Before you contact a professional, familiarize yourself with what the project will likely entail. Buy a home-repair book. Go to the library and spend some time on the Web. Most important, talk to others who have had similar work done. You want to know what to ask, which materials are involved, how much the project could cost, and what the variations might be if you go with different materials or construction. Ask why a bid is low or high. You will learn a great deal on the fly as you listen to professionals, so take plenty of notes.

As you bring people in to give estimates, it may be helpful to prepare a standard list of questions (see the following pages for suggestions), so that you can be sure you are comparing bids fairly (apples to apples versus apples to oranges) and that you obtain the necessary details to make an informed decision. Also, be sure to check all names of final contenders with the Better Business Bureau and remember to never disclose to one professional the competing bids of others.

Time and again, homeowners find themselves wishing they'd done their homework more thoroughly. Remember to ask references not only whether they were happy with the final result, but what they might have done differently, how long it took, whether it came in on budget and on time. Check older projects as well as more recent ones, as a shoddy job may not reveal wear and tear right away.

Finally, plan to be as easily available as possible whenever any kind of work is being done on your home. You'll want to be able to answer questions and supervise how the work is being done.

QUESTIONS TO ASK PROFESSIONALS

- Do they have liability insurance?
- Are they licensed and bonded?
- Do they have worker's compensation?
- What are the payment terms?
- What is the schedule?
- Will they draw up a written agreement with a detailed description of the work to be done?
- Will they provide a list of references?
- Will they be on site for the entire duration of the project?

QUESTIONS TO ASK REFERENCES ABOUT A PROFESSIONAL

- Would they recommend this person? Why or why not?
- Were the estimated cost and schedule accurate?
- Was the level of craftsmanship what they had hoped for?
- Has it held up well?
- Was the person on site for the entire duration of the project?
- Was the person honest and pleasant to work with?

DO-IT-YOURSELF > If you are considering embarking on a project yourself—large or small—read on.

Be realistic before you embark on any project. Some do-it-yourself projects are easy, others difficult, labor-intensive, or dangerous. When it comes to electrical repairs, it is best not to get involved with wiring unless you really know what you are doing, because faulty wiring could present a significant fire danger. The same goes for major plumbing projects: Although some projects can be done easily, don't dive into a complicated project unless you know what you are doing. Small repairs—fixing a leaky faucet and such—are fine, but water damage can be an expensive risk to take.

Remember that do-it-yourself projects are not free. Some require highly specialized tools that you might never need again. Although you can rent some tools, be realistic about how long it will take a novice to do the job versus professionals who are experienced and own their own tools. This holds true especially if you are renting a complicated piece of machinery by the hour.

Also keep in mind that contractors get wholesale discounts, so do the math carefully. Consider the following example: You want to insulate your attic; you buy the insulation at full retail, buy the safety mask, gloves, goggles, and the specialized blade with which to cut it, and install it yourself at great length and discomfort, only to find out that a pro could have gotten a significant discount on materials and done the whole thing more quickly. In addition, he would have known how to insulate around the beams so as not to interfere with ventilation (something you would have had to learn)—a job that, if done incorrectly, might cause moisture to accumulate and your roof to rot. You may have saved yourself little money, lost a lot of time, and caused some damage in the process.

Consider carefully how long you think a job will take and what your time is worth. It is often said that home-improvement projects take three times as long as you think they're going to. You will only frustrate yourself if you are unrealistic ahead of time about what will be involved. Keep in mind that the bulk of a job may take half the time, but it may take half again as much time to finish the project's details, moldings, or awkward edges. Also remember that you have to set aside time for proper setup and cleanup. Many people live for months and even years with "almost finished" projects. They've pulled up the carpet, but have yet to install the floors. They've redone the floors, but just have not had time to reinstall the baseboards. Do one project at a time, start to finish, then move on.

Finally, ask yourself whether you have the necessary skills. Your home is an investment. Over the long term, it's not worth doing a poor job of it. If you plan to sell, you want your home to look right, and if you plan to stay, you don't want the repairs to come apart. Be honest with yourself about what you know and don't know—and about what you need to know. What is worth learning over the long term: how to fix a leak, which will come up again and again, or how to complete a project you will only do once?

If you are unsure about whether you want to proceed, the worksheets that follow will help you evaluate the various considerations to keep in mind. If you are confident that you can do it yourself, then they can help you plan your budget and timing.

hiring a professional: worksheet

PROJECT:

DETAILED DESCRIPTION OF WHAT I WANT >

_____

_____

_____

_____

_____

WHAT WILL NEED TO BE DONE TO ACHIEVE IT >

_____

_____

_____

_____

_____

WHO DOES THIS KIND OF WORK >

_____

_____

_____

LEVEL OF SKILL REQUIRED >

_____

_____

QUESTIONS TO ASK >

_____

_____

_____

_____

_____

_____

bids

VENDOR NO. 1

company name >

contact >

address >

phone >

e-mail >

web site >

referred by >

total bid >

notes >

VENDOR NO. 2

company name >

contact >

address >

phone >

e-mail >

web site >

referred by >

total bid >

notes >

VENDOR NO. 3

company name >

contact >

address >

phone >

e-mail >

web site >

referred by >

total bid >

notes >

VENDOR NO. 4

company name >

contact >

address >

phone >

e-mail >

web site >

referred by >

total bid >

notes >

CONCLUSION (WHOM I'VE CHOSEN AND WHY) >

reference checks

REFERENCE NO. 1

name >

phone >

e-mail >

would they recommend vendor >

notes >

REFERENCE NO. 2

name >

phone >

e-mail >

would they recommend vendor >

notes >

REFERENCE NO. 3

name >

phone >

e-mail >

would they recommend vendor >

notes >

TIPS: Be sure to get the following from your final contender.

evidence of liability insurance ❑
evidence of license ❑
payment terms ❑
schedule ❑
written agreement ❑
estimated cost ❑

Also ask if your contact will be present on the job site.

final details

PAYMENT TERMS >

SCHEDULE >

ESTIMATED COST:
FINAL COST:

NOTES >

hiring a professional: worksheet

PROJECT:

DETAILED DESCRIPTION OF WHAT I WANT >

WHAT WILL NEED TO BE DONE TO ACHIEVE IT >

WHO DOES THIS KIND OF WORK >

LEVEL OF SKILL REQUIRED >

QUESTIONS TO ASK >

bids

VENDOR NO. 1

company name >

contact >

address >

phone >

e-mail >

web site >

referred by >

total bid >

notes >

VENDOR NO. 2

company name >

contact >

address >

phone >

e-mail >

web site >

referred by >

total bid >

notes >

VENDOR NO. 3

company name >

contact >

address >

phone >

e-mail >

web site >

referred by >

total bid >

notes >

VENDOR NO. 4

company name >

contact >

address >

phone >

e-mail >

web site >

referred by >

total bid >

notes >

CONCLUSION (WHOM I'VE CHOSEN AND WHY) >

reference checks

REFERENCE NO. 1

name >

phone >

e-mail >

would they recommend vendor >

notes >

REFERENCE NO. 2

name >

phone >

e-mail >

would they recommend vendor >

notes >

REFERENCE NO. 3

name >

phone >

e-mail >

would they recommend vendor >

notes >

TIPS: Be sure to get the following from your final contender.

evidence of liability insurance ❑
evidence of license ❑
payment terms ❑
schedule ❑
written agreement ❑
estimated cost ❑

Also ask if your contact will be present on the job site.

final details

PAYMENT TERMS >

SCHEDULE >

ESTIMATED COST:

FINAL COST:

NOTES >

hiring a professional: worksheet

PROJECT:

DETAILED DESCRIPTION OF WHAT I WANT >

_____

_____

_____

_____

_____

WHAT WILL NEED TO BE DONE TO ACHIEVE IT >

_____

_____

_____

_____

_____

WHO DOES THIS KIND OF WORK >

_____

_____

_____

LEVEL OF SKILL REQUIRED >

_____

_____

QUESTIONS TO ASK >

_____

_____

_____

_____

_____

_____

_____

bids

VENDOR NO. 1

company name >

contact >

address >

phone >

e-mail >

web site >

referred by >

total bid >

notes >

VENDOR NO. 2

company name >

contact >

address >

phone >

e-mail >

web site >

referred by >

total bid >

notes >

VENDOR NO. 3

company name >

contact >

address >

phone >

e-mail >

web site >

referred by >

total bid >

notes >

VENDOR NO. 4

company name >

contact >

address >

phone >

e-mail >

web site >

referred by >

total bid >

notes >

CONCLUSION (WHOM I'VE CHOSEN AND WHY) >

reference checks

REFERENCE NO. 1

name > _____

phone > _____

e-mail > _____

would they recommend vendor > _____

_____

_____

notes > _____

_____

_____

REFERENCE NO. 2

name > _____

phone > _____

e-mail > _____

would they recommend vendor > _____

_____

_____

notes > _____

_____

_____

REFERENCE NO. 3

name > _____

phone > _____

e-mail > _____

would they recommend vendor > _____

_____

_____

notes > _____

_____

_____

_____

TIPS: Be sure to get the following from your final contender.

evidence of liability insurance ❑

evidence of license ❑

payment terms ❑

schedule ❑

written agreement ❑

estimated cost ❑

Also ask if your contact will be present on the job site.

final details

PAYMENT TERMS >

_____

_____

_____

SCHEDULE >

_____

_____

_____

ESTIMATED COST:

FINAL COST:

NOTES >

_____

_____

hiring a professional: worksheet

PROJECT:

DETAILED DESCRIPTION OF WHAT I WANT >

WHAT WILL NEED TO BE DONE TO ACHIEVE IT >

WHO DOES THIS KIND OF WORK >

LEVEL OF SKILL REQUIRED >

QUESTIONS TO ASK >

bids

VENDOR NO. 1

company name >

contact >

address >

phone >

e-mail >

web site >

referred by >

total bid >

notes >

VENDOR NO. 2

company name >

contact >

address >

phone >

e-mail >

web site >

referred by >

total bid >

notes >

VENDOR NO. 3

company name >

contact >

address >

phone >

e-mail >

web site >

referred by >

total bid >

notes >

VENDOR NO. 4

company name >

contact >

address >

phone >

e-mail >

web site >

referred by >

total bid >

notes >

CONCLUSION (WHOM I'VE CHOSEN AND WHY) >

reference checks

REFERENCE NO. 1

name >

phone >

e-mail >

would they recommend vendor >

notes >

REFERENCE NO. 2

name >

phone >

e-mail >

would they recommend vendor >

notes >

REFERENCE NO. 3

name >

phone >

e-mail >

would they recommend vendor >

notes >

TIPS: Be sure to get the following from your final contender.

- evidence of liability insurance ❏
- evidence of license ❏
- payment terms ❏
- schedule ❏
- written agreement ❏
- estimated cost ❏

Also ask if your contact will be present on the job site.

final details

PAYMENT TERMS >

SCHEDULE >

ESTIMATED COST:

FINAL COST:

NOTES >

hiring a professional: worksheet

PROJECT:

DETAILED DESCRIPTION OF WHAT I WANT >

WHAT WILL NEED TO BE DONE TO ACHIEVE IT >

WHO DOES THIS KIND OF WORK >

LEVEL OF SKILL REQUIRED >

QUESTIONS TO ASK >

bids

VENDOR NO. 1

company name >

contact >

address >

phone >

e-mail >

web site >

referred by >

total bid >

notes >

VENDOR NO. 2

company name >

contact >

address >

phone >

e-mail >

web site >

referred by >

total bid >

notes >

VENDOR NO. 3

company name >

contact >

address >

phone >

e-mail >

web site >

referred by >

total bid >

notes >

VENDOR NO. 4

company name >

contact >

address >

phone >

e-mail >

web site >

referred by >

total bid >

notes >

CONCLUSION (WHOM I'VE CHOSEN AND WHY) >

reference checks

REFERENCE NO. 1

name >

phone >

e-mail >

would they recommend vendor >

notes >

REFERENCE NO. 2

name >

phone >

e-mail >

would they recommend vendor >

notes >

REFERENCE NO. 3

name >

phone >

e-mail >

would they recommend vendor >

notes >

> **TIPS:** Be sure to get the following from your final contender.
>
> evidence of liability insurance ❑
> evidence of license ❑
> payment terms ❑
> schedule ❑
> written agreement ❑
> estimated cost ❑
>
> Also ask if your contact will be present on the job site.

final details

PAYMENT TERMS >

SCHEDULE >

ESTIMATED COST:

FINAL COST:

NOTES >

hiring a professional: worksheet

PROJECT:

DETAILED DESCRIPTION OF WHAT I WANT >

_____
_____
_____
_____
_____

WHAT WILL NEED TO BE DONE TO ACHIEVE IT >

_____
_____
_____
_____
_____

WHO DOES THIS KIND OF WORK >

_____
_____
_____

LEVEL OF SKILL REQUIRED >

_____
_____

QUESTIONS TO ASK >

_____
_____
_____
_____
_____
_____

bids

VENDOR NO. 1

company name >

contact >

address >

phone >

e-mail >

web site >

referred by >

total bid >

notes >

VENDOR NO. 2

company name >

contact >

address >

phone >

e-mail >

web site >

referred by >

total bid >

notes >

VENDOR NO. 3

company name >

contact >

address >

phone >

e-mail >

web site >

referred by >

total bid >

notes >

VENDOR NO. 4

company name >

contact >

address >

phone >

e-mail >

web site >

referred by >

total bid >

notes >

CONCLUSION (WHOM I'VE CHOSEN AND WHY) >

reference checks

REFERENCE NO. 1

name >

phone >

e-mail >

would they recommend vendor >

notes >

REFERENCE NO. 2

name >

phone >

e-mail >

would they recommend vendor >

notes >

REFERENCE NO. 3

name >

phone >

e-mail >

would they recommend vendor >

notes >

TIPS: Be sure to get the following from your final contender.

evidence of liability insurance	❑
evidence of license	❑
payment terms	❑
schedule	❑
written agreement	❑
estimated cost	❑

Also ask if your contact will be present on the job site.

final details

PAYMENT TERMS >

SCHEDULE >

ESTIMATED COST:

FINAL COST:

NOTES >

hiring a professional: worksheet

PROJECT:

DETAILED DESCRIPTION OF WHAT I WANT >

WHAT WILL NEED TO BE DONE TO ACHIEVE IT >

WHO DOES THIS KIND OF WORK >

LEVEL OF SKILL REQUIRED >

QUESTIONS TO ASK >

bids

VENDOR NO. 1

company name >

contact >

address >

phone >

e-mail >

web site >

referred by >

total bid >

notes >

VENDOR NO. 2

company name >

contact >

address >

phone >

e-mail >

web site >

referred by >

total bid >

notes >

VENDOR NO. 3

company name >

contact >

address >

phone >

e-mail >

web site >

referred by >

total bid >

notes >

VENDOR NO. 4

company name >

contact >

address >

phone >

e-mail >

web site >

referred by >

total bid >

notes >

CONCLUSION (WHOM I'VE CHOSEN AND WHY) >

reference checks

REFERENCE NO. 1

name >

phone >

e-mail >

would they recommend vendor >

notes >

REFERENCE NO. 2

name >

phone >

e-mail >

would they recommend vendor >

notes >

REFERENCE NO. 3

name >

phone >

e-mail >

would they recommend vendor >

notes >

TIPS: Be sure to get the following from your final contender.

evidence of liability insurance	❑
evidence of license	❑
payment terms	❑
schedule	❑
written agreement	❑
estimated cost	❑

Also ask if your contact will be present on the job site.

---

final details

PAYMENT TERMS >

SCHEDULE >

ESTIMATED COST:

FINAL COST:

NOTES >

hiring a professional: worksheet

PROJECT:

DETAILED DESCRIPTION OF WHAT I WANT >

_____
_____
_____
_____
_____

WHAT WILL NEED TO BE DONE TO ACHIEVE IT >

_____
_____
_____
_____
_____

WHO DOES THIS KIND OF WORK >

_____
_____
_____

LEVEL OF SKILL REQUIRED >

_____
_____

QUESTIONS TO ASK >

_____
_____
_____
_____
_____
_____

bids

VENDOR NO. 1

company name >

contact >

address >

phone >

e-mail >

web site >

referred by >

total bid >

notes >

VENDOR NO. 2

company name >

contact >

address >

phone >

e-mail >

web site >

referred by >

total bid >

notes >

VENDOR NO. 3

company name >

contact >

address >

phone >

e-mail >

web site >

referred by >

total bid >

notes >

VENDOR NO. 4

company name >

contact >

address >

phone >

e-mail >

web site >

referred by >

total bid >

notes >

CONCLUSION (WHOM I'VE CHOSEN AND WHY) >

reference checks

REFERENCE NO. 1

name >

phone >

e-mail >

would they recommend vendor >

notes >

REFERENCE NO. 2

name >

phone >

e-mail >

would they recommend vendor >

notes >

REFERENCE NO. 3

name >

phone >

e-mail >

would they recommend vendor >

notes >

TIPS: Be sure to get the following from your final contender.

evidence of liability insurance ❑
evidence of license ❑
payment terms ❑
schedule ❑
written agreement ❑
estimated cost ❑

Also ask if your contact will be present on the job site.

final details

PAYMENT TERMS >

SCHEDULE >

ESTIMATED COST:

FINAL COST:

NOTES >

hiring a professional: worksheet

PROJECT:

DETAILED DESCRIPTION OF WHAT I WANT >

WHAT WILL NEED TO BE DONE TO ACHIEVE IT >

WHO DOES THIS KIND OF WORK >

LEVEL OF SKILL REQUIRED >

QUESTIONS TO ASK >

bids

VENDOR NO. 1

company name >

contact >

address >

phone >

e-mail >

web site >

referred by >

total bid >

notes >

VENDOR NO. 2

company name >

contact >

address >

phone >

e-mail >

web site >

referred by >

total bid >

notes >

VENDOR NO. 3

company name >

contact >

address >

phone >

e-mail >

web site >

referred by >

total bid >

notes >

VENDOR NO. 4

company name >

contact >

address >

phone >

e-mail >

web site >

referred by >

total bid >

notes >

CONCLUSION (WHOM I'VE CHOSEN AND WHY) >

reference checks

PROJECT:

REFERENCE NO. 1

name >

phone >

e-mail >

would they recommend vendor >

notes >

REFERENCE NO. 2

name >

phone >

e-mail >

would they recommend vendor >

notes >

REFERENCE NO. 3

name >

phone >

e-mail >

would they recommend vendor >

notes >

TIPS: Be sure to get the following from your final contender.

evidence of liability insurance ❏
evidence of license ❏
payment terms ❏
schedule ❏
written agreement ❏
estimated cost ❏

Also ask if your contact will be present on the job site.

final details

PAYMENT TERMS >

SCHEDULE >

ESTIMATED COST:

FINAL COST:

NOTES >

do-it-yourself: worksheet

PROJECT:

WHAT IS INVOLVED (setup, dismantling, priming or prepping, renovation itself, finishing touches, reassembling, cleanup, etc.) >

_____

_____

_____

_____

EST. NO. OF HOURS REQUIRED > _____

ESTIMATED SCHEDULE (HRS. / WEEK) > _____

DEADLINE > _____

TOOLS REQUIRED >

_____

_____

_____

_____

COST OF RENTAL / PURCHASE >

_____

_____

_____

_____

MATERIALS REQUIRED >

_____

_____

_____

_____

COST OF MATERIALS >

_____

_____

_____

_____

SAFETY EQUIPMENT REQUIRED >

_____

_____

COST OF RENTAL / PURCHASE >

_____

_____

EST. TOTAL COST:

NOTES >

_____

_____

_____

do-it-yourself: worksheet

PROJECT:

WHAT IS INVOLVED (setup, dismantling, priming or prepping, renovation itself, finishing touches, reassembling, cleanup, etc.) >

EST. NO. OF HOURS REQUIRED >

ESTIMATED SCHEDULE (HRS. / WEEK) >

DEADLINE >

TOOLS REQUIRED >

COST OF RENTAL / PURCHASE >

MATERIALS REQUIRED >

COST OF MATERIALS >

SAFETY EQUIPMENT REQUIRED >

COST OF RENTAL / PURCHASE >

EST. TOTAL COST:

NOTES >

do-it-yourself: worksheet

PROJECT:

WHAT IS INVOLVED (setup, dismantling, priming or prepping, renovation itself, finishing touches, reassembling, cleanup, etc.) >

_____
_____
_____
_____

EST. NO. OF HOURS REQUIRED > _____

ESTIMATED SCHEDULE (HRS. / WEEK) > _____

DEADLINE > _____

TOOLS REQUIRED >

_____
_____
_____
_____

COST OF RENTAL / PURCHASE >

_____
_____
_____
_____

MATERIALS REQUIRED >

_____
_____
_____
_____

COST OF MATERIALS >

_____
_____
_____
_____

SAFETY EQUIPMENT REQUIRED >

_____
_____

COST OF RENTAL / PURCHASE >

_____
_____

EST. TOTAL COST:

NOTES >

_____
_____
_____